A CROW'S DREAM

ALSO BY DOUGLAS VALENTINE

The Hotel Tacloban (1984)

The Phoenix Program (1990)

TDY (2000)

The Strength of the Wolf: The Secret History of America's War on Drugs (2004)

The Strength of the Pack: The Personalities, Politics, and Espionage Intrigues That Shaped the DEA (2009)

A CROW'S DREAM

POEMS

BY

DOUGLAS VALENTINE

THE OLIVER ARTS & OPEN PRESS

Valentine, Douglas, 1949 -
A Crow's Dream
Poetry by Douglas Valentine
ISBN: 978-0-982-987-8-6-5
Library of Congress Control Number: 2011942345

The Oliver Arts & Open Press
2578 Broadway, Suite #102
New York, NY 10025
http://www.oliveropenpress.com

CONTENTS

A CROW'S DREAM

I

A Crow's Dream

In the dream
You were hiking up a high hill on a forested trail.
The crow was flying beside you
And you were looking up at the crow in the trees.
You were saying you were happy
— that you were happiness —
And knew things about happiness you could say.

When you reached the rocky summit
You cradled your staff in your arms.
You were bare-shouldered,
And your words were swept away by the high winds.
You turned around, facing away,
And your bare white back became part of the cliff —
And the crow flew off the mountain side
Over the trees, into my dreams.

Off the Trail

We walked off the trail, long into the woods,
And stopped in a patch of feathery ferns.
We sat on a log, breathing fragrant air,
And I swooned, and fell, in a turn.

The forest wrapped around me like fog,
The only sound I heard was your voice,
Calling me out from my slumber
To a world of infinite choice.

Had you left me on your shoulder,
Had you hummed a sweet lullaby,
Glad would I have stayed forever,
Far from the hiker's watchful eye.

Crane Hill

She arrived at my door tired
From her trek through the knee-deep snow.

Breathing hard
She pulled off her mittens
And unwrapped her scarf
While I fetched her coffee
The way she likes it:
Black, with a shot of whiskey.

She leaned forward in the chair
In front of the stove
Warming her hands on the steaming cup.

"The oak atop Crane Hill was glowing gold tonight,"
She said.
"When I passed under it
A branch came around from behind in the dark
And touched me on the shoulder,
Right here."

Shivering, she sat up straight.

"When I turned and looked
It seemed to clutch the stars."

This woman knows where the running pine
Grows green beneath the snow,
And every time she comes
I wonder how I'll die...
Or if I'll know.

The Shamrock Café

"Late in my last life."

This is how it often begins
Concentrating on my words
A conversation across the bar.

"My life here is a mystery:
It's like coming full circle."

If someone were to check my ID
They'd find I was too young
To be playing this game,
Making it up as I go along.

Four Corners

An old bum tosses an empty quart bottle of beer,
Wrapped in a brown paper bag, into a vacant lot.

A little kid who has just learned to totter
And whose mother speaks French
Pulls the bottle from the bag and flips it
Casually over the curb into the street
Where it shatters into a hundred sharp pieces.

A tall slim girl in a black leotard
And a long white skirt
Moving fast on rollerblades
Past the cars parked on the street
Does a quick split to avoid the broken glass
Spins in a full circle to a standstill -
Stopping just short of a jogger who ran the red light -
Claps her hands once above her head
And shoves off happily on her way.

Memorial Day

I'm standing on a sidewalk
In Pleasantville, New York. It's 1959
And I'm holding the American flag in my hand.

It's really hot in the bright sunshine,
But I stand at attention like a good soldier
And salute my father, who smiles and waves
In this home of the free, this land of the brave.

Dad's with the World War Two veterans. They're marching to the beat
Of the fire department band sweeping down the street:
The horns blare, the drums pound, the cymbals crash -
And my consciousness cracks like shattered glass.

The band's overtaken by soaring boys on bikes.
Their spokes are woven with red white and blue crepe paper
And the fluttering streamers on their handle bars
Make them look like firecrackers on wheels.

It's so damn dazzling I have to look away,
Down at my feet, and I'm starting to sway
From the glare reflecting off the concrete.
I squint, and swoon, and look up at the sky
Where the light on the leaves of the sugar maple trees
Reflects off the chrome of the cars on the street.
I'm breathless, and dizzy, and overdone.
The one thing I know, this isn't fun.

"Don't you ever let that flag touch the ground!"
Snaps a mean old man, twisting my arm up so it hurts.

Disapproving town folk stare.
I feel their looks in the depths of my soul.
What else can a ten year old boy do but slink away
And chuck that fucking flag over the first privet hedge?

It was there and then that I knew that being
A good citizen was too much responsibility
For anyone as weak and as young as me.
To this day my favorite part of the Memorial Day Parade
Is the sound of the street cleaner
Pushing the star spangled flakes of confetti
Into his pan and pouring them,
With a soft sweet swoosh, into his pail.

Nui Ba Den
(For Jack Madden)

Five miles east of Cambodia,
Solitary in a vast steaming plain,
That huge magnetic rock is riddled
With caves, VC tunnels, and graves:
To the pilgrims waiting to ascend
It is a sacred place: Nui Ba Den.

I traveled through ten thousand lives
To reach that cold Saturnian mass —
That point of departure from the past —
Where an irresistible will
Momentarily ruled my world
Till I was arrested by souls of the dead.

Nui Ba Den: The Black Virgin Mountain
Inaccessible from a squalid cell in Tay Ninh.
My passport held, accused of being a spy,
I bribed my way free —
Only to regret my exalted liberty.

Shadow Land

A freckled girl with tangled hair
Dances in a sun-splashed field of grass
Oblivious to the buzzing bees
Twirling barefoot in a rumpled dress -
Imagining herself.

Her world is a blur around her:
The forsythia hedge, her house on the hill,
The soaring locust trees and the ancient ash
With its one impossible branch -
Upon which sits an observant boy.

Third Eye

Her first eye is a diamond
Star bright
Guiding me through brush
And tangled vines
To her mouth.

Her second eye is a ruby
Drawing me inside -
Sparks light my way
Flames lick at
Her teeth.

Her third eye is sapphire
Shadowed water
Spring fed from
Her cold
Throat.

At Forest Park

I saw the great blue heron at his place
By the pond, and I saw a fawn,
And a hummingbird flew next to me
While I was doing my Le Gong.

The cones on the Norway spruce
Are speckled gold against green:
At Forest Park, on a clear day,
They are the greater part of me.

All Things Pass

Filtered somehow through patterned hours
We measure now our opening eyes
By light showers of their Sabric sunrise
And the afternoon is always ours.

We share a conversation on the porch
Before us an ancient blue sea spreads wide
The new moon summons the essential tide
Between us the light of a living torch.

Our spirit, caught in crystalline air,
Is cleansed and calm, our vision clear.
All things pass before us here.
All things pass before us here.

The Way

Somewhere between what is
And where one most wants to be
She asks not what once was true
Questions not where one has been
Nor why, but here and now
Moves as far away as one would go
Matching her companion step for step
Her aura blue skies
Fanning yellow flames.

We dance in silence along jeweled streets
Which, like our dreams, spin away forgotten.

Across the vastness of space
Are pools of light
And pockets of cool shadow.

The way has opened to me.

I have sat with her
On the edge of the universe
Our legs dangling over the side
Void of superstition.

The Ball Knows The Way

A languid summer day
In the woods we cleared into fields
Making our own rough course.

We stood atop a tree-studded hill
Overlooking a trout pond:
Our fourth hole.

I dropped a golf ball on the ground
And pointing at a gap in the tree tops, said
"I shall hit this ball through that hole, into the pond."

And with my trusty seven iron and fluid swing, I did.
And to prove it was no fluke
I did it again.

Smiling, I turned to Chris and said
"Do I think the ball on its way?
Or does the way open up to me?"

"Neither," he said matter-of-factly.
"The ball knows the way."

The Modern World

There is more light
In the world today
Than ever before.

In fact, there is
No dark side to
The planet anymore.

In Las Vegas I wait
In the middle of the night
For the last word
On electricity.

Building a Wall

The wall is tangible: I balance my life with stones
Placing weight and size where they achingly go,
Digging back and down in the gravely sand,
No flourishes, no feints, no slights of hand.

icicles

I have heard
lovers touch
like crickets

ceaseless through
the night
yet with a

jeweled sound
of icicles
and a blue

tinted image
of you in
love with me

wishing wells

window panes

weather vanes

tinted glass

bending grass

wishing wells

chest swells

eye lids close

wind blows

magic dust

covers us

faces in the stream

faces in the stream
among passing clouds

have never been so near
or so far:

the look in their eyes
is lost in the time it takes
to give a name.

The Frozen River

After four weeks of unbroken freeze
The Contoocook River is an avenue of ice,
Save for a narrow stream coursing down its center:

Could I fold it open like a book along that spine
It would tell a tale that roared and flowed in spring.

--

Through a drafty window filled with frost
I watch starlings stand in a dotted line
And drink from that dark stream:

Could I see clearly, I might learn of their hard
Existence here, in lettered tracks on snow.

--

Time slows into silence at the river bend.
Ghostly columns of frozen mist arise,
The essence from under and within:

They stand among the bare trees on the hillside
And shiver when they catch the hollow light.

--

Hallowed black and white world in mid-winter,
Empty and complete on this muted day,
The sun a phantom orb behind the clouds:

Pale grey as the paper hornets' nest that hangs
From the level oak branch on the bank.

The First Snow

The clouds had been gathering,
Growing darker and lower all morning long.

I sat on the trunk of an oak I'd cut down:
I was tired but relaxed, feeling strong.

I was warm, though the cold air stung my face.
My senses were sharp:
I was totally aware of that place.

Not a breath of wind was blowing
When the clouds touched the tree tops
And the first flakes began to fall
Evenly among the branches,
White against brown,
Like a beaded curtain coming down.

My Last Spring

I shall not be in this
My last spring
I swear on my soul
The same ancient thing.

I'll start in morning the usual way
Bursting from the green tipped hazel
In red blossoms soaking the ground –
Escaping at the seams from the grasp
Of ghosts and recurring dreams

Arising like a field of uncatalogued herbs
With healing force, a new gender of verbs
That describe an utterly new action of me
Apart from the past, painless, free.

I shall not be in my last spring
Some ancient withering thing -
And though I start the usual way
I shall not sleep at end of day.

Easter Sunday

I was half a step away
My foot was raised
When I heard the dry leaves rustle.

In the tall grass tumbling
Down the south side of the hill,
From under a loose, flat stone,
Three baby snakes poked out their heads
And flashed their forked tongues
On Easter Sunday morn.

The first slithered off,
And the second submerged.
But the third turned its neck
Like a crooked finger and fixed me
With a cold accusing eye.

Redwing

The scene is always the same:
I'm intruding in someone else's dream,
Someone much older
With white hair, pointing
A stick at a bird in a tree.

The moon, of course, is waxing.

Icicles sweet with syrup
Drip from maple branches.

Beyond the split rail fence
Someone slips into the forest.

It's always over too soon
Before I think it through -
Before I remember how
To glide like the redwing
Without ceremony
Across the thawing fields.

How to Prune an Apple Tree

When pussy willows glisten with dew
And maple buds are turning red
And the moon, of course, is waxing -
In early spring, before it blossoms white -
That's the time to prune an apple tree.

It's far easier then than in the fall
When it's weighted down with fruit
And far healthier for the tree.

First remove the suckers from the trunk
And then, if it's an old neglected tree,
Remove one or two of the bigger branches:
Open it up inside – let it breathe –
But leave no gaping holes.

Whatever's left after that
Gets shaped to what's left.

From within the heart and looking out,
It should seem as if green summer leaves
Are evenly spaced against blue sky.

Last, take a step back and walk all around.
The rest of the job gets done from out here
With a pole pruner and hand snips,
Crawling in occasionally,
Balancing,
And touching up.

Viburnums

All around me are thoughts
Of things that might happen soon:
It's mid-August and seems like
It's been raining since June.

I was pruning the crab apple tree
When a red-bellied woodpecker shot by
Like an otter under ice, over the roof
To its hole in the dead elm out back.

I brought the ladder into the garage,
Concerned with every green leaf in the yard;
I saw years of labor, of unfulfilled dreams,
Swirling on the hard north wind.

In mid-August the tall viburnums are over-laden
With flat clusters of red berries;
They bend so far, they seem about to break.
My heart aches with the weight of their branches,
And I realize my mistake.

Rebels

We sat in a mosquito infested swamp
Listening to Radio Free Somalia.

The mercenary we caught,
A former Marine from Texas,
Took it well...but talked.

We have a little piece of
The action in Atlantic City:
Jersey is a good place to
Turn cash and buy guns.

We have little else:
Just this hot spot
And next year's news
Coming over the box.

Rice and Rubies

No one knows all of Burma
but we know this much:
rice and rubies.

And giant ferns
like huge green fans,
and a blue bird that shrieks
through a yellow beak,
mocking man.

The Burmese give us rubies,
and we give them rice.

Blackness and Ruby

It was easy to be lost
among sedge and alder,
where the green heron hides,
worshipping sun and corn
and a woman with wings.

Out of the riverbank marsh,
what do I recall of her now?

Her blackness and ruby.

How glad I was to wrench myself
from the sycamore's trunk,
and fling myself into the fire
that burns in her crypt;

How simple it was to follow,
speaking in tongues,
surrendering.

The Abandoned House

Wild boys tore the wallboards off,
And one by one knocked the bricks
From the crumbling chimney.

It was a place to smoke and read girlie magazines,
Among fallen tar paper shingles
And the clinging stench of creosote.

At first they were afraid of getting caught,
Of being seen by some prying adult;
But only one family lived further down
The dirt road, beyond the bend, and they were
Indians (they said) or Negroes (said everyone else)
And didn't look, and couldn't complain -
And the old farmhouse across the road was out of sight,
Hidden by an ancient apple orchard.

But mostly they were afraid of ghosts,
Of violent vagabonds hiding outside;
Afraid of that mysterious heap of rusty cans
In the driveway overgrown with weeds,
Left by someone much wilder than them.

The Attic Voice

As a child I heard the attic voice
Calling to me more softly
Than a field of moonlit grass
More softly than your sigh upon my chest.

It was scorching hot and dry
A narrow passage arched by
Splintered wooden rafters
Draped with cobwebs
And studded with rusty nails.

Quickly back down the stairs
Latching the attic door
A vow to return when older.

Clean Sheets

I'm sorry
But the trouble with you Mom
I swear
Is that you talk but never listen.

And you always knows what's
Right and wrong.

Maybe I should be more like you
And apologize before I begin.
Better yet....

Mom! I've got good
Attendance thanks to you
And thanks for the hot breakfast
And thanks for the clean sheets.

But Mom
I know I never said this before –
And I don't want to hurt your feelings
Like I always do –

But I'm not coming home.

San Francisco

When it was time to get out
I dropped everything
and ran.

But I could never get out far enough –
so I took a vow of poverty
on Mission Street.

There was something free and hot to eat
once a day, downtown
at St. Anthony's,

And a priest scornfully handed out
sandwiches behind the church across
from Washington Park.

While scavengers ate crumbs off plates in coffee shops,
I sold blood once a week
on Market Street -

Leaned against a hard building off one of those steep streets,
short of breath,
passing out.

There I began a career of walking round the block,
walking round the clock,
with nothing to say.

I stood on the corner of Broadway and Grant
at four am,
alone,

And stopped on moonlit Montgomery at dawn,
the only life not withdrawn
into stone.

A newspaper truck rattled by
and I thought - I shall
name this world.

II

The Hand Is Faster Than The Eye
(Composed 11 September 2001)

I learned that lesson long ago,
It was the first articulated truth:
"The hand is faster than the eye,"
Said the raven to the youth.

There is love, and then betrayal.
There is a cause, and then there's none.
Then Mandrake lifts his velvet cape
And all you ever knew is gone.

Superstition

Danny held a bottle of cheap red wine
In a brown paper bag, and summed up our situation:

"Whoever opens the bottle releases an evil spirit,"
He said solemnly, quoting his Apache grandmother,
"And must empty the bottle, so the evil spirit within
Does not escape into the world, and harm others."

So we consumed the devil and he was in us
And would have his way that night in Anaheim,
Tempting us, for we were poor,
And without coin.

We sat with our backs against the concrete wall
Of the all-night liquor store, drunk, our legs
Stretched loosely out across the sidewalk,
Knowing a fate worse than jail awaits the man
Who cannot finish what he has begun.

And we probably would have robbed that store,
Had we not been too drunk to find Danny's gun.

Mimic of the Truth

Sometimes I wonder if you can keep our secret
For to mimic the truth would make a fool of it
And you might forget how to hold your peace.

Could I dance and sing for others as I do for you?
Or pull my hair and rave without acting poorly?

I hear you chanting in your cave tonight:
Your words scorch the sky like shooting stars
Tumbling in the desert
Meteors down in powdery sand
Impregnating the land
With troubled ghosts, echoes and mirages.

Give some sign that you may yet
Remain in somnolent search
Behind boulders and opiated fog
Among lizards and scorpions.

Leave your faithless entourage.
Make sooth this lacunar dream.

My Foolish Death

I closed my fingers 'round the blade
And laid the handle in your palm
Less true than proud or unafraid.

With bandaged hand and trailing blood
I bypassed friends in town and fled
To your cave where the dark stream ends.

Laughing, you took me in your arms,
Knowing that with my final breath
I would confess my love
And beg forgiveness for my foolish death.

Fear of the Future

To those eating acorns
And huddled around the fire,
The man at the mouth of the cave
Seems tangled in the stars.

In his left hand he shakes a leafy branch
And with his right, he throws stones at the moon.

Through want and hard hunger
They gnaw at bones, suck marrow,
Lick dew off grass, eat roots,
And turn their eyes from the sun.

Lawn Party

Above a scented garden Japanese
Lanterns sway in the evening breeze
Strung between porch and fence and trees.

Summer creatures paper thin
Each about to burst in flame
Too delicate to contain.

In shadows across the lawn
A foreign party drifts
Beneath an arch of terrestrial gifts.

Random Events

A surly man hits his thumb with a hammer
(Freud would say it was no accident
That he secretly dislikes himself)
Curses and in a blind rage kicks his dog.

His faith in mankind shattered
The dog weaves and sniffs his way down the street
And bites a neighbor's spoiled child on the leg.

You are that spoiled child.
You call it cause and effect.
Your critics say it is the law of attraction.

God claims the incident had nothing to do with Him:
He observed the whole thing, but at a safe distance.
He says, like everything else, the bite was attributable to
The universal law of random events.

No secret there.

The Woods

The sound of a stray
companion is the abrupt
sweep of a swollen stream.

Something draws near....
the rhythmic patter
of the tapering rain.

One faint whistle, then another:

As soon as seen gliding
through the foggy meadow,
the redwing vanishes in the trees.

Evening wanders in alone
drifting more slowly with
each breath of the wind.

Just as likely you shall pass these damp leaves
as it is to search these woods for you.

Just So

A yellow corpse lies in a furrow in a field,
Its deep intuitions and faded superstitions
Figments of fair-haired imagination —
Haunted, dressed in forest green, licking dew
Off blades of grass...and beckoning.

Wouldn't it be something if that's the way it really is?
Everyone dreaming all the time
Making things out to be something they're not
Trying to look just so
To make it all seem right.

Pristine World

The sun rolls across
an emerald sea
in a pristine world.

The exact god
who shaped this sphere
made it even
at the poles and rimmed its girth
with swaying palms.

Two parakeets flitter
atop one feathery frond,
catching the light
on the tips of
their green and yellow wings.

Deciding to Adopt

Not being able to have a father of my own
I have decided to adopt.
But the store doesn't have any to spare
So it looks like I'll have to take a mother instead.

On second thought....If I can't have a father,
I won't have parents at all —
I'll live alone, if necessary, or get married.

A Writer's Résumé

I've written five books
But haven't read any of them.

Before I wrote I climbed trees for a living.
It was how I overcame my fear of heights.

The owner of the tree company used to say:
"Self praise is no recommendation."

Indeed. And thus, in his honor, this résumé
Is no longer about my many accomplishments.

I've written five books and plan to write one more:
If you're interested, it will have all the details.

Talent

Talent is a beautiful girl.
When you're with her, people notice.
But she bangs on your door at odd hours
And disappears for long stretches,
And has no patience for your wife,
Your children, your dull friends.

She is thrilling indeed,
But some day she will leave you for good.
And one night, after she's been gone for years,
You will see her on the arm of a younger man,
And she will pretend you don't exist.

Ramada Rendezvous

We meet in the motel lounge outside town
And she makes small talk about him:
He drinks too much and thinks she's taking
Acting lessons tonight, playing Desdemona.

And indeed she is deep in a drama.

I am Saturnine in my obsession with her sex:
Her penetrating eyes, blazing,
Sear the base of my spine.

We quickly take the stairs to the room
Undress without words and sit on the bed.
I could not see her even if I looked
For she has been annihilated.

My hand under her and in between her
Drives her back, deeper into oblivion.
She is no longer afraid or ashamed.

Later we stand beside her car
In the parking lot, outside again,
Two ghosts looming in the glow of a streetlamp
Making another appointment with death.

Sober Patty

Sober Patty lives by the book.
Straighten her life out anymore
And she'd be the bottom line.

This is an old friend talking
The one she left at the Ramada –
The one with no idea where to look.

"It wasn't the Ramada," she says.
"Not there. I'd remember."

She doesn't have to worry,
I'm not telling.
Or am I?

Sober Patty is ticklish about zero
Because it makes her toes curl
And takes her mind off mathematics.

Route 9A

I hitched a ride down 9A from Poughkeepsie
To Briarcliff with a fat truck driver.

His cigar smoke and opinions mingled in the cab
While he poked around inside my soul.

"Going home to see your girl?" he asked.
"Afraid she's fucking someone else?"

He was wearing a wife-beater T-shirt,
Delivering produce to market in New York City.

When I jumped out at the traffic light he said wickedly:
"It's her belly. She can put anything she wants in it."

That didn't change anything
And he knew that too.

Dante's County Fair

Put your dime down and spin the wheel
And hope it stops on something real:
It's preordained, it's in the air,
Here at Dante's County Fair.

Different Things

The nickel spinning on the counter top
Is an indecisive dime disputing heads and tails.

"We're talking about two different things."

It wanders as it spins between
An ashtray and a glass of beer —
Until a finger from above
Deftly stops it on its edge.

The Cat

Curled in a rectangle of light
Her silver-tipped fur glistens
As she travels like a cloud
Across the room
At the laconic speed of the sun
Spanning the morning sky —

Yawning, stretching,
Slipping into another warm pool
On the carpet, with no ambition
Save an appointment with warmth.

Dolphins

Dolphins in a playland pool
Will eventually throw
Themselves on the ground
And drown in the air.

Same with leopards in the zoo:
They climb to the tippy tops of
Their phony trees and leap.

If you have enough money
You can buy any animal a name
And make it do tricks in Texas.

You Never Know

It's late in December, there's a snap in the air,
The sky's steel grey, the fields are as white as her hair.

These days it's hard to get out and travel around -
Everywhere you try to go there's ice on the ground.

And they're predicting sleet, but it just might snow:
Like anything else, you never know.

Grow Two Additional Heads

"Grow two additional heads,"
The blue man said forcefully,
"And I shall tell you the secret of the dragon."

So I stomped the red earth
Four times, mumbled a prayer,
And did what I was told.

"Fine," the blue man said,
Then vanished in a cloud of smoke
Leaving behind a pile of burnt ashes.

"So much for making queries of a phoenix,"
Said my green head to my gold.

Plaster Walls

Could it be these plaster walls enclose the same room
we stumbled through yesterday
searching in closets and drawers
in envelopes and books?

Who would have thought that heaven was so near?
Did we expect a glowing red and gold palace
or some misty orchard in Arcadia long ago?

A simple sip of water has loosened my soul
in summer, at the height of day.

Brook Violets

I have seen in summer in the yellow wood
brook violets you have woven
with thread drawn from a rainbow.

I have sipped the bright sunshine you held for me
in a cup of green leaves.

Blinded by the firelight of your body
I have heard you play upon the silken strings of dawn
in tune with all growing things

And felt your snowflake fingers settle soft on my soul
while your kisses closed the deep-sea eyes of song.

Love

My thoughts hover just above my reach
and though I wish to bid them farewell
I would as soon not gaze at the moon
nor honor the stars in night's dark heaven:
and always, love, must you return.

The Gentle Touch

We face each other across the sea
shared tension dissipating
within the widening
immeasurable shores
until the loneliness of each is lost within
and once again we become
the gentle touch
reaching itself.

Love I Knew Not

Love I knew not what you said
being from a distant world.
By chance we met on common soil -
we were two and therefore strange.

It being this place and some time
only made it more coincidental.

And your love was no doubt true
though falsified with words
spoken in a foreign tongue
to one not then in love.

Still I Have Trouble

Still I have trouble
not spilling the newly
filled ice cube tray.

Such matters of balance
escape my talents
when tilted this way.

So on this crooked course
of late I force myself
to drink it straight.

III

Unreasonable Faith

"Unreasonable faith becomes you,"
The master said,
"And mute endurance."

Come to Naught

A thought about thought
come to naught.

The Everlasting Enjambment

I

It is said that intellectuals and those in love
Cannot meditate.

It has to do with iambic pentameter,
Ten syllables being the length of the average English breath.
And etymology:
The origin of the word breath is found in Germanic "bhreu,"
Meaning exhalation.

Breath to the Latin was inspiration: "spirtitus."
And what is inspiration other than the human mind
Contemplating the absurdity of its death?

Consider the emptiness in between the stars
That so terrified Frost.

I'm not asking you to intellectualize -
And of course, if you're in love,
You just don't care.

What I'm asking you to consider
Is the space between exhalation and inhalation,

Wherein you find a pebble, a blade of grass, a deer:
A four by four by eight foot woodpile, or a jar in Tennessee:

A fisherman's net, or an 18 inch opening in a fence -
18 inches being the breadth of the average English chest,
Mediating between man and nature, casting spells.

Our cultural etymology makes it clear that
After college, and before the poem, comes

The everlasting enjambment, infinite after out,
Before the (not so) inevitable in.

II

We find this place amusing, but then again,
We find everything funny.

It's in our genes, our own peculiar genealogy,
Suspended between empire and antiquity,
Oscillating between sun and shadow,
Whistling through all these graveyards.

And it is absurd, standing alone at the center of space and time,
Like Christ nailed on the cross.

We are icebergs subject to heat and cold,
Floating within the everlasting enjambment.

III

I got all the lights going through town.
We'd been discussing Ashbery
And what he was trying to say, if anything.

Hirshfield said he was a "language" poet
Concerned with giving voice to our modern thought processes.

This, from someone who never got a rejection letter,
About someone who can't seem to say what he means.

Well, just because she said it, doesn't mean it's true.
Maybe Ashbery was trying to say a lot of things.

And who cares that he was inspired by a grown man
Sitting like a cartoon character at a toy piano,
Imitating the sound of
The everlasting enjambment.

I got all the lights going through town
But they were paving the highway,
And that slowed me way down.

IV

Marvis Flynn

A Poem in Three Parts

I

Un Petit Mal

The dark stream slips tonight through an error
    In the arrangement of these trees,

Seeps in between and swells over the fallen rocks
    Of the roadside wall marking his way.

Outside him in circles it spreads a moonlit pool
And stills his passage along these cobbled stones.

How much of all that seems certain
    Could vanish with a word?

The Night

The night steps
Slowly with age

A reminder of when
We were fully grown.

Monarch of forest and fire
Of stream and gray stone

Retracing ancestral lines
To an appointment with light.

The City

He came in the rain in the night
And left before dawn.

Our FatherWho art in Heaven, borrowed be Thy Name

Marvis Flynn would stay awake waiting.
He slept during the day.

Thy boredom come, Thy will be dumb

His mother packed quickly and they moved
To this City in the West.

On earth as it is in prison

His father has another wife here
And six other children.

Give us this day our daily dread

Marvis Flynn does not know his sister
Until his father sees them together hand in hand.

*And forgive us our trespasses as we forgive those
Who do nothing at all*

His father tells them who they are
And they part in confusion.

*And lead us into temptation
And deliver us unto evil*

The New Rex Hotel

Marvis Flynn wanders off Broadway into an alley
  Where he kneels and coughs blood.

Emptied of life, he strides up starlit stairs,
  Stairs littered with trash and broken glass

Up to the second floor
Of the New Rex Hotel.

He reads the numbers above each door
Each door on either side of the hall.

Sign On The Door:

I have smoked Haba in Knaba
Kief in the street
And opium in the den:
Never once have my words been engulfed
In any Neptunian fog.

The Pool Hall Connection

Idle Chinese men sit amid curling cigarette smoke.
Thin crooked fingers sculpt the wax paper

Skin that clings to their faces.
Seated against the wall in sullen silence

They watch the players bare their souls.
Cadillac Jack speaks to one like something in himself.

Later...

Marvis Flynn gulps mouthfulls of pills on the roof
Sees diamonds in the sidewalk below

Sees white sheets snap on a clothesline on a roof across the street
Rising on the wind, revealing the full moon

Revealing the contours of the man in the moon
The moon man on the outskirts of the City

Where freight trains are swallowed whole
By invisible curves in the tracks

Their whistling sound caught
In tangled trees.

Cadillac Jack

Marvis Flynn gets up to go
Feels a chill at the door
Takes a step back.

Cadillac Jack in a Panama hat says
"I got forty-four white Cadillacs,
El Dorados and Broughams and more.
Forty-four white women, unnerstand?
Star bitches all
Cause I'm certified, bonafide
And qualified to slam Cadillac doors.

Why, I lines the bitches up in the mornin'
And has'em drop their drawers for inspection, unnerstand?
Then I slaps' em all right down the line
With one swipe of my hand:
And there's one fourteen year old bitch
With platinum hair and red lips smiling up at me.
So I reaches into my pocket
Pulls out of roll of stick matches
Strikes 'em across her teeth
Lights a big cigar
Blows the smoke in her face and says
Bitch, don't you smile at me unless you got money, unnerstand?
If you gotta turn one trick for one dollar
For one hour till you earn a hunner'd dollars
Don't ever smile at me."

Marvis Flynn bends his head down
And a bit to one side

From the corner of one eye he watches
Cadillac Jack watch him as he walks away

The shadow of an ailanthus tree
Cast by a streetlight over his shoulder

Grows in the night past his marching feet
As he descends into concrete.

Balancing Act

Balancing as best he can, Marvis Flynn
Tip-toes along the curb outside a basement bar.

Peering through a window he sees Claudia inside
Pressing her body against Cadillac Jack's.

Jack's finger slides down her spine
Tracing its path with a blood-red nail.

Her mother went to sleep with a clothespin on her nose.
She wanted to marry a millionaire.

Bloodlets trickle from a hundred pin-pricked
Holes in her arms, her legs, her feet, her hands

Her dreams escaping into the
Stream of traffic outside

Drifting as far as dreams can go
In the last gray hour before dawn

Unwinding through a maze of factories
Warehouses and deserted streets

They sweep through the City
Escorting Marvis Flynn

Beyond the seven storefront sleepers
As far downtown as he dares to go

Where no moon guides the heart
And no wind blows

Where cats see better than men
And few claim night vision.

Claudia

The hurricane circled round and round
Without wind or rain or sound.

Claudia sits in the center of the room,
Her blue-veined hands folded gently in her lap.

Cadillac Jack stands behind her,
His fingers stroking her silken hair.

Having approached on bended knee, Marvis Flynn
Sacrifices his empty words to the air.

Claudia says to him:
"You are too late.
There is no reason
For you being here."

—

Claudia lies on her back on the floor,
Her hips moving slowly, legs spread wide

The sun through the window at dawn
Caressing her smooth white thighs

Her soft sigh a suggestion
That the Light has betrayed him.

Looking through the wind's eye
Marvis Flynn sees the crow fly.

Lyrical Ballad

In Chinatown in Chinatown
The fish rot in the street

While at Saint Anthony's shelter
There's something hot to eat.

Meatless Friday was in hip pocket
All the time, but

Like circles and stars, some things
Are never where they seem to be

So Marvis Flynn learns to ignore the facts,
And removes himself from belief.

Coming True

Marvis Flynn flips on the overhead light in his room
Sits on a wooden chair and stares at his hands:

What was never said might have mapped a plan
Might have spared him from a memory

But what is never said leaves no mistake
And nothing asked leaves nothing unanswered.

Marvis Flynn is heir to a curse
Of walking the same path every day

Without assurance of bird song or church bell
With no familiar voice to give him pause

He no longer laughs at a world
He will all too quickly join.

Marvis Flynn has wandered far from home
His purposes have dimmed

There is no evidence of his being born
No passport to verify his presence

There is only the rarity
Of his coming true.

The Light

The glare from the bulb in the ceiling
Shakes his trembling hands beyond his grip.

He knows this is no deer path in the woods
Winding through ancient buried cities

He knows this is no caravan route
To Kublai Khan in Xanadu.

From his chair he sees cigar store
Indians spread across the desert

And shipwrecked sailors adrift
In this parched billboard land.

No longer able to recall his port of call
Marvis Flynn looks and sees only sand.

Empty-handed in mad circles
About his being loose

Tight-lipped in the wide swing
Of his wild pursuit

Eyes shut tight against the rush
Of all forgotten things

Pulled by his hair, his head bent back,
Marvis Flynn stares into the light.

II

The New World

The echo of a heartbeat is all that remains
Of their passage across the trackless earth:

In this manner the Romans with their maps in hand
Tip-toed o'er the ocean to the New World

Crushing those Antediluvian peaks
Beneath the sparkling blue.

Up sprang the mushrooms of Atlantis
Their orange and purple in the wooded green.

This was before the stars knew orchestration
When the wind blew unpredicted through the leaves.

The Eternal Return

The wind becomes more articulate
And time has less to say

As each layer of skin is pulled away
Each memory-dulling potion drained.

Dismembered with a sword in hand
In search of an adjective to precede the man

He writes upon her chalk white thighs with blood
That nothing makes sense but sensation

That no amount of strength of arm
Can stretch the stem or make it grow

Can turn the leaf from green to gold
As her sea green eyes turn to gray.

Marvis Flynn would be insane and live beyond
Any meaning these words might convey

He would live beyond the sum
Of all the pain he has known or caused.

He has become his own invention
Intentions undone

He has returned his wasted body to the earth
He has already sung.

III

Change

Today a music box and a robin's egg
Tomorrow a chestnut bowl
Yesterday Persian carpets and a flowerpot

Each day brings change
Seldom real magic

Today your portrait
Tomorrow porcelain tile in a labyrinth design
Yesterday, goldfinches and a grandfather clock

Each day brings change
Seldom real magic.

Mad Together

The eyelashes of morning
Brush against his cheek

The fog lulls him back to sleep
Its cool breath on his neck.

Claudia sleeps well dressed
Keeps lilies in a hat beside the bed.

She sits on the bed cross-legged
And cares less about lasting than becoming.

Knowing nothing more of remarks
Marvis Flynn bows at her altar

Serving her with his tongue
Successively.

Living with her now
They dress up but never go out

And he thought she would have more to say
Than simply repeating

"We shall go mad together."

True Love

They meet on a narrow path
Face one another and find it hard to pass

Yet in their random orbiting
They cross again and again

On a path too narrow
To walk side by side

Outstretched arms are for balance
Eyes are for looking ahead

And should one chose to turn
Then one must follow

Encountering the simple real
Chaos stenciled on perception

Spots of cold
Streams of warmth

The monotony of God
The illogic of love

A hint of "I know"
An echo of "Me too."

Learning to Fly

Like a morning on the Mediterranean
His life fans out away from the day.

Born of sunlight and sea breeze
It is the tapping of feet when the music is done.

Marvis Flynn wraps the pieces of himself in a blanket
And wonders what form this change will finally take.

Day joined to day wed to night
He finds himself trying to paint

A picture of himself on canvas
Not a house in the country

Not red or green or blue,
He lives in the space

Between his hand and eye
Making dreams come true.

Time

The tree falls and lands
In a clearing in the woods.

The machine dismantled and cleaned
Reassembled runs more smoothly.

Men fishing with long poles
Horseshoe crabs in the sand

Drawbridges and whirlpools
Make sense of this unsettled world.

He sees more clearly the pain in her eyes
Reflected down this corridor of mirrors

To the center of time
To the core of what they need

That they stand apart
Certain that they share one self

Certain that time will not erase
The sense that binds them now.

A Walk In The Woods

Marvis Flynn on a walk in the woods
Discovers snow in May -

Old snow crusted with dirt and tangs
With pockets of air inside -

Old snow of spring wet against his knees
In the shade beneath a hemlock tree.

He screws his fist into the sharp chill
Opens his hand and sings

"Claudia of the Sky,
Only the pheasant's eye

Can see your adolescent red
Against this hoary white.

Claudia of the Rain,
It took forever

To find you on this
Walk in the woods."

But not as long as the lily
Lasts in the vase

Not as long as the flame
Stands still on the wick.

The End

The flame is still on the candle
The flowers are still in her hat

Ghosts drift across the wall
Three triangles touch

Claudia whispers
"There is no room at the top of the stairs."

Yet she stands in the doorway
Wider than the surface of the earth

Siphoning the full moon's oracles
Into a language he can speak

The constellations in her wild blue eyes
Tell him what is hidden behind the wheel

Then she gives him to drink
That he might recall

That he too walked across the desert
Pockets full of sand

Leaving a trail of lost hours
Compelled to look behind.

Flight

Rising from her chair, Claudia
Steps to the window and opens it

Outside, a path spins
Through a yellow wood

To a clearing where
A crow settles on a branch.

Rising from his chair
Hovering in the air

His breast a field
Of wind-rustled feathers

Marvis Flynn flies away.

Coda

The curtains inhaled by the evening wind
Let the last few sparks of sunlight in.

On his table a deck of cards
Spreads apart as wide as chance.

He draws the Fool and knows it's true
That puppet strings at her command

Not Marvis Flynn
Have moved his hand.

CPSIA information can be obtained at www.ICGtesting.com
Printed in the USA
BVOW081933231212

308959BV00004B/32/P